The life cycle of a

Cat

Ruth Thomson

Published in 2013 by Wayland
a division of Hachette Children's Books, an Hachette UK
Company
www.hachette.co.uk

British Library Cataloguing in Publication Data
Thomson, Ruth
The life cycle of a cat. - (Learning about life cycles)
I. Cats - Life cycles - Juvenile literature
I Title
571.8'19752

Editor: Victoria Brooker
Designer: Simon Morse
Senior Design Manager: Rosamund Saunders

Printed and bound in China

Wayland
Hachette Children's Books
338 Euston Road, London NW1 3BH

Wayland Australia
Level 17/207 Kent Street
Sydney NSW 2000

Photographs: Cover main image, 4–5 Blickwinkel/ Alamy; 2 Ulrike Schanz/naturepl.com; 6, 7, cover inset centre, 16, 22, 23 Aflo/ naturepl.com; 8, 23 Bartussek/ ARCO/ naturepl.com; 9, 10, 12, 13, 14, 15, 17, 18, 23 Jane Burton/naturepl.com; cover inset top, cover inset bottom, 11, 19, 23 Wegner/ ARCO/naturepl.com; 20 and 21 Bengt Lundberg/naturepl.com

ISBN: 978-0-7502-7187-5
10 9 8 7 6 5 4 3 2 1

Contents

Cats live here

Most cats live with people in their homes. People feed and look after cats and give them a warm place to sleep.

What is a cat?

Pet cats belong to the animal family that includes wild cats such as lions. All cats are meat eaters. They can run fast or **stalk** silently on their soft **paws**.

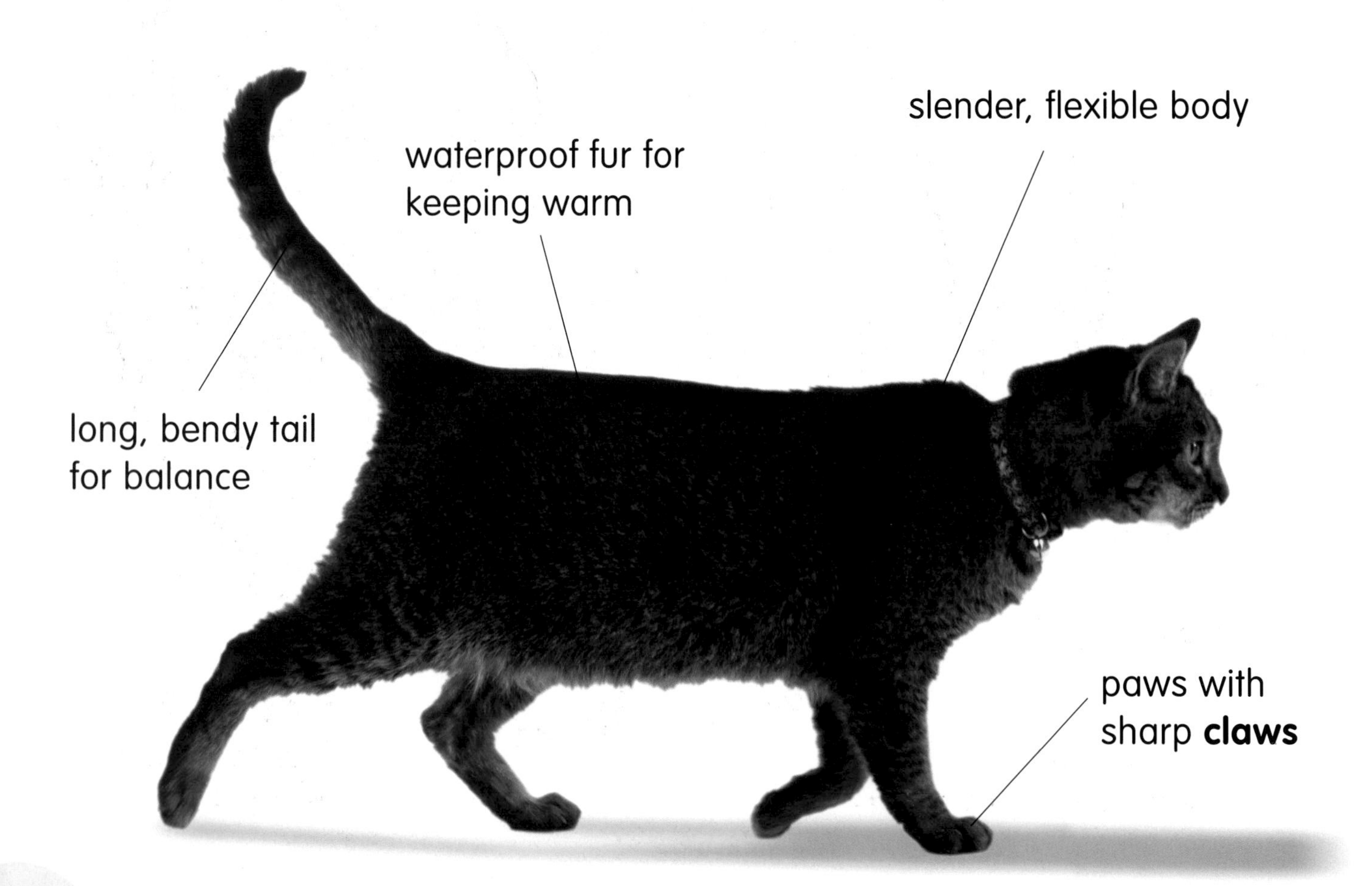

Cats have very sharp senses.

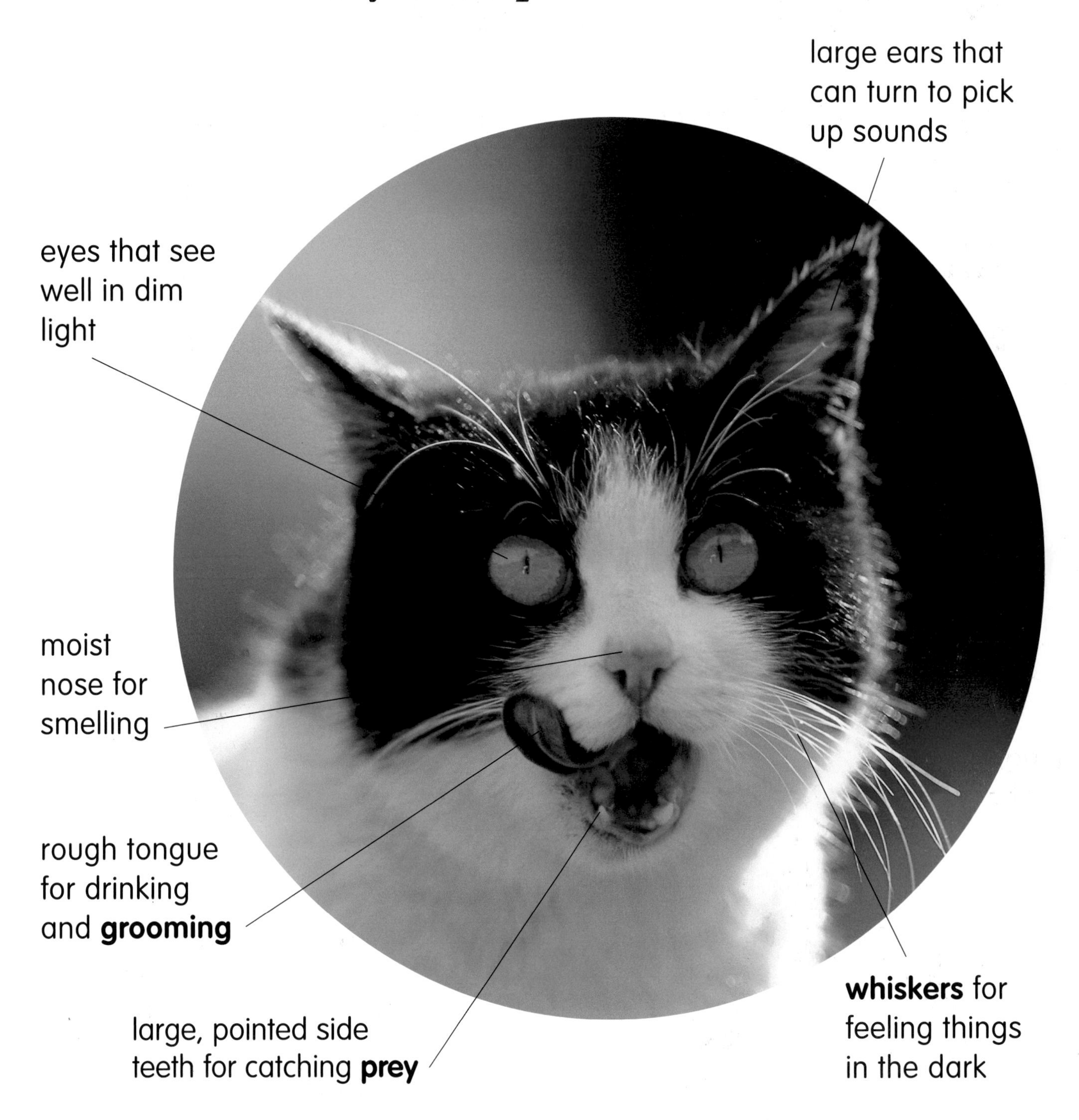

Birth

A mother cat gives birth to a **litter** of four or five kittens. The newborn kittens are tiny and damp. Their mother licks them dry.

A newborn kitten is weak and helpless. It cannot see or hear, and it has no teeth.

Its legs are floppy and its **claws** stick out from its **paws**.

Baby kittens

The kittens snuggle up to their mother to keep warm. They **suckle** on her milk. Each kitten chooses a **teat** and always suckles on the same one.

1
day

The mother begins to leave her kittens for a short while. The kittens sleep in a heap. They keep each other warm while their mother is away.

10 days

Walking

After a week or so, a kitten's eyes and ears open. But it takes a few more days before the kitten can see or hear well. It can crawl about, but wails if it cannot find its mother.

Soon the kitten is strong enough to stand and take its first steps.

Growing up

The kittens begin to grow teeth. Then they can start eating kitten food and drinking water.

The kittens become very curious.
They sniff everything.
They tap objects.
They have play-fights.

Learning

The kitten learns from its mother how to **groom** itself. It licks its front **paw** and wipes it across its face and ears. It twists its head to groom the side of its body.

The mother cat helps her kittens learn hunting skills.
She waves her tail as if it were a moving **prey**. The kittens **stalk** and pounce on it.

Playing

The kittens become bolder and stronger. They love playing. They watch a toy on a string and leap into the air to grab it.

9 weeks

The kittens like to climb everywhere. They use their **claws** to grip.

Going outside

As the kittens grow older, they like spending time outside. They climb trees, find sunny spots to sleep and may chase mice or birds.

By six months, the kittens are young cats. They like to wander as they please. They can always find their own way home.

1 year

Adult cat

Cats are fully grown when they are a year old. Now they can produce kittens of their own.

Cat life cycle

Birth
The mother cat gives birth to four or five kittens.

1 week
The kittens spend all day suckling or sleeping.

2-3 months
The kittens play, explore and learn to hunt inside and outside.

1 year
Cats are fully grown and can have kittens of their own.

Glossary

claw a long curved, pointed nail at the end of an animal's **paw**

groom to clean by licking or pulling through fur

litter a family of baby animals born at the same time

paw an animal's foot

prey the animals that are killed by other animals for food

stalk to hunt an animal quietly trying to keep hidden

suckle to feed on milk from a mother

teat the part of a female animal that its babies suck to get milk

whiskers the long, stiff hairs on the face of a cat

Index